The GOSPEL for CHILDREN

A simple, yet complete guide to help parents
teach their children the Gospel of Jesus Christ

JOHN B. LEUZARDER

ILLUSTRATIONS BY REGINA ORR

Shepherd Press

First edition in September 1996 by Calvary Press, P.O. Box 805, Amityville, NY 11701
ISBN 10: 0976758288
        13: 9780976758280

Second edition in February 2002, by Shepherd Press Inc., P.O. Box 24, Wapwallopen, PA 18660, © 2002.

Scripture quotations are from the New International Version (NIV), © 1994 International Bible Society.

Layout: Richard Ouellette

For information address the publisher :
Shepherd Press Inc
P.O. Box 24, Wapwallopen, USA
PA 18660
Telephone: (800) 338-1445
www.shepherdpress.com

Leuzarder, John B., 1996-2002
        The Gospel for Children / by John B. Leuzarder; illustrated by Regina Orr   p. cmé
        Summary: A colorful well illustrated book to be used by parents or teachers to teach Children the Gospel of Jesus Christ.
        ISBN 0-9663786-8-7

        Recommended Dewey Decimal Classification: 234
        Suggested Subject Headings:
        1. Religion—juvenile literature—teaching literature. 2. Christianity—juvenile literature—teaching literature. 3. The Bible—juvenile literature—teaching literature.
        I. Title

ACKNOWLEDGEMENTS

I would like to thank the following people for their contributions
which assisted in the creation of
The Gospel for Children:
Pastor David Johnson whose sermon spurred the idea for this book.
J.I. Packer, whose book Evangelism and the Sovereignty of God
(published by Inter-Varsity Fellowship) helped form a basic outline
from which to work.
Pat Schuessler for her help and creativity in preparing the manuscript.

CONTENTS

PREFACE

Many of us are familiar with the term "Gospel". We have hopefully heard its message in sermons, tracts or on TV. We understand its great importance because God's Word tells us that the Gospel "is the power of God for the salvation of everyone who believes" (Romans 1:16). Understanding this, then, we would all agree that offering this message about the saving work of Jesus Christ to our children, as soon as they are able to grasp its meaning, is of utmost importance.

But where do we start? The Gospel is far more than a few lines out of a tract. In fact, to properly comprehend the Gospel we must reasonably understand all that the Bible teaches about the nature and character of God, about man as a created being, his fall into sin and his desperate condition, as well as the work of Jesus Christ to save men from God's wrath and eternal punishment. We also need to understand what God expects of His redeemed people and what it means to be an heir to the glories of eternal life.

This book has been written to aid parents, teachers and guardians in teaching children the essential doctrines of our faith. It accomplishes this by organizing foundational biblical truths in a way that can be understood by children 5 years old and up. A **Gospel Summary** that consolidates truths found in the book into a more concise message is also included.

As a father of two young daughters, I sought to find a book that would assist me in conveying the Gospel to my children. None could be found. Over a period of 18 months I worked on a format that would capture my girls' youthful interest, be complete, doctrinally correct, and lend itself to being hidden in their hearts. The result is the book before you, now in its second edition and printed in three languages.

We thank our loving Savior for the enablement and privilege of preparing this work for His honor and glory.

John Leuzarder

HOW TO USE THIS BOOK

This book has been designed to provide a way for parents and teachers to hide the essential elements of the Gospel message in the hearts of children ages 5 years and older. It does so by categorizing foundational biblical truths in a simple outline form, using colorful illustrations to capture interest and facilitate recall. The format has proven to be conducive to instruction, interaction and memorization. Used as a teaching tool or in daily devotions, the book encourages children to remember and understand the **Main Outline Points**.* Youngsters have fun testing their recall using the **Memory Helps** found in the back of the book.

If you choose to have your child memorize the material, may we suggest that you consider providing an incentive in the form of a reward to encourage the child to successfully memorize the six chapter headings and 38 outline points. Our children were asked to explain each point in their own words, showing that they comprehended the meaning, prior to receiving a reward. It took each of our daughters (at 6 years of age) about 3 to 4 weeks to accomplish this.

Under each outline point are biblical truths supporting it. These, along with the Bible references and illustrations, can be used in discussion and interaction with the child to further enhance their understanding of the Main Outline Point. We suggest that you work with your child on one chapter at a time, before moving on.

Although some words in this book are challenging for young children, we have been pleasantly surprised to see how quickly the meanings have been grasped when explained patiently.

May God bless you richly as you bring His Word to bear upon the hearts of children.

example:

Main Outline Point *
(to be learned)

No one is as great as God[1] **
• God is self existent and depends on no one else.[2]
• God is all-powerful and all-knowing.[3]
• God always was and always will be.[4]
• He is perfect and has never made a mistake or done anything wrong.[5]

Supporting Truths
(for discussion)

Memory Help Illustrations
(see end of book)

** Supporting biblical texts corresponding to these numbers are found at the end of each chapter.

GOD

No one is as great as God[1]

- God is self existent and depends on no one else.[2]
- God is all-powerful and all-knowing.[3]
- God always was and always will be.[4]
- He is perfect and has never made a mistake or done anything wrong.[5]

God created all things[6]

- In 6 days God created the universe and everything in it from the smallest cell to the largest mountain.[7]
- God loves all He has created.[8]

God controls everything each day[9]

- Nothing is too small or insignificant to escape His notice.[10]
- He causes or permits things to happen that we like and things that we don't like.[11]
- He provides our food, clothes, shelter, and other things we need.[12]
- We depend on Him to keep our heart beating, to make the sun come up in the morning, and to take care of everything else in our lives.[13]

God created each of us[14]

- He decided who our parents would be, when and where we would be born.[15]
- God gave us souls that can never die.[16]
- God created us for His own glory.[17]

We belong to God[18]

- God owns us.
- He requires us to live for His glory and will.[19]

As His creatures He commands us to *obey* Him[20]

- We must learn to obey His teachings.[21]
- We are to love Him with all our heart, mind, spirit and strength, and love our neighbor as ourselves.[22]

7

He commands us to *worship* Him[23]

- By talking to Him daily in prayer.[24]
- By living pure and righteous lives for Him.[25]
- By praising Him in words and song.[26]
- By coming together with other Christians to learn His Word, worship and praise Him.[27]

He commands us to *serve* Him[28]

- By cheerfully, carefully and quickly carrying out our responsibilities.[29]

He commands us to *glorify* Him[30]

- By telling others what He has done for us.[31]
- By bringing honor to Him by living so that others can see that we love and obey God in everything we do.[32]

BIBLE REFERENCES

1   Psalm 89:5-8 "The heavens praise your wonders, O Lord, your faithfulness too in the assembly of the holy ones. For who in the skies above can compare with the Lord? Who is like the Lord among the heavenly beings? In the council of the holy ones God is greatly feared. He is more awesome than all who surround Him. O Lord God almighty, who is like you?" Also Rom 11:33-36, Psalm 147:4-5, Psalm 8

2   John 5:26 "For as the Father has life in himself, so he has granted the Son to have life in himself."

    Acts 17:25 "And he is not served by human hands, as if he needed anything, because he himself gives all men life and breath and everything else."

3   Daniel 4:35 "He (God) does as He pleases with the powers of heaven and the peoples of the earth. No one can hold back his hand or say to him: "What have you done?"

    Heb 4:13 "Nothing in all creation is hidden from God's sight. Everything is uncovered and laid bare before the eyes of Him to whom we must give an account." Also Psalm 76:4-12, Job 38:4-6, Luke 1:37; Psalm 139:1-4

4   Psalm 90:2 "Before the mountains were born or you brought forth the earth and the world, from everlasting to everlasting you are God. Also Jer 10:10; I Tim 1:17

5   Matt 5:48 "Be perfect, therefore, as your heavenly father is perfect." Also Deut 32:4

6   Neh 9:6 "You alone are the Lord. You made the heavens even the highest heavens, and all their starry host, the earth and all that is on it, the seas and all that is in them. You give life to everything and the multitudes of heaven worship you." Also Gen 1:1; Col 1:16; Psalm 89:11.

7   Exodus 20:11 "For in six days the Lord made the heavens and the earth, the sea, and all that is in them."

    Also Gen 1:1-2:3; Heb 11:3

8   Psalm 145:17 "The Lord is righteous in all His ways and loving toward all He has made." Also John 3:16.

9   Isa 46:9-10 "I am God, and there is no other; I am God, and there is none like me. I make known the end from the beginning, from ancient times, what is still to come. I say: My purpose will stand, and I will do all that I please." Also Prov 16:9; Eph 1:11; Psalm 139:16.

10 Matt 10:29-30 "Are not two sparrows sold for a penny? Yet not one of them will fall to the ground apart from the will of your Father. And even the very hairs of your head are all numbered."

11 Acts 14:17 "He has shown kindness by giving you rain from heaven and crops in their seasons; he provides you with plenty of food and fills your hearts with joy."

    Psalm 71:20-21 "Though you have made me see troubles, many and bitter, you will restore my life again, from the depths of the earth you will again bring me up. You will increase my honor and comfort me once again.

    Also I Peter 1:3-9; Job 1:21

12 Psalm 145:15-16 "The eyes of all look to you, and you give them their food at the proper time. You open your hand and satisfy the desires of every living thing." Also Psalm 136:25; Acts 14:17

13 Col 1:17 "He is before all things, and in Him all things hold together." Acts 17:28 "For in Him we live and move and have our being." Also Matt 5:45; Dan 2:21

14 Psalm 139:13 "For you created my inmost being; you knit me together in my mother's womb." Also Isa 43:6-7

15 Acts 17:26-27 "From one man he made every nation of men, that they should inhabit the whole earth; and he determined the times set for them and the exact places where they should live."

16 Matt 10:28 "Do not be afraid of those who kill the body but cannot kill the soul. Rather, be afraid of the One who can destroy both soul and body in hell." Also Eccl 12:7; Rev 6:9-11

17 Isa 43:6-7 "Bring my sons from afar and my daughters from the ends of the earth – everyone who is called by my name, whom I created for my glory, whom I formed and made." Also Rev 4:11

18 Eze 18:4 "For every living soul belongs to me, the father as well as the son – both alike belong to me."

Also Deut 10:14

19 Matt 7:21 "Not everyone who says to me, 'Lord, Lord,' will enter the kingdom of heaven, but only he who does the will of my Father who is in heaven."

Isa 43:7 "Everyone who is called by my name, whom I created for my glory." Also I Cor 10:31

20 Lev 18:4 "You must obey my laws and be careful to follow my decrees. I am the Lord your God."

John 15:10 "If you obey my commands, you will remain in my love, just as I have obeyed my Father's commands and remain in his love." Also Eph 5:1-6

21 John 14:23-24 "Jesus replied, 'If anyone loves me, he will obey my teaching. My Father will love him, and we will come to him and make our home with him. He who does not love me will not obey my teaching. These words you hear are not my own; they belong to the Father who sent me.'" Also Deut 6:4-7; John 15:10

22 Mark 12:30-31 "'Love the Lord your God with all your heart and with all your soul and with all your mind and with all your strength.' The second is this: 'Love your neighbor as yourself.' There is no commandment greater than these."

23 Psalm 29:2 "Ascribe to the Lord the glory due his name; worship the Lord in the splendor of his holiness." Also Psalm 100; Matt 4:10

24 Eph 6:18 "And pray in the Spirit on all occasions with all kinds of prayers and requests." Also Rom 12:12; Psalm 100; Psalm 105:2

25 2 Cor 7:1 "Since we have these promises, dear friends, let us purify ourselves from everything that contaminates body and spirit, perfecting holiness out of reverence for God." Also Matt 5:8; Rom 12:1

26 Psalm 105:1-3 "Give thanks to the Lord, call on his name; make known among the nations what he has done. Sing to him, sing praise to him; tell of all his wonderful acts. Glory in his holy name; let the hearts of those who seek the Lord rejoice."

27 Col 3:16 "Let the word of Christ dwell in you richly as you teach and admonish one another with all wisdom, and as you sing psalms, hymns and spiritual songs with gratitude in your hearts to God." Also Heb 10:25

28 Eph 6:7 "Serve wholeheartedly, as if you were serving the Lord, not men." Also Deut 11:13; I Peter 4:10

29 Col 3:23-24 "Whatever you do, work at it with all your heart, as working for the Lord, not for men, since you know that you will receive an inheritance from the Lord as a reward. It is the Lord Christ you are serving."

2 Cor 9:7 "Each man should give what he has decided in his heart to give, not reluctantly or under compulsion, for God loves a cheerful giver."

30 John 15:8 "This is to my Father's glory, that you bear much fruit, showing yourselves to be my disciples." Also Psalm 105; Isa 43:7

31 Luke 8:39 "'Return home and tell how much God has done for you.' So the man went away and told all over town how much Jesus had done for him." Also Psalm 105:1-2

32 Matthew 5:16 "In the same way, let your light shine before men, that they may see your good deeds and praise your Father in heaven." Also I Peter 4:11

WRITE DOWN YOUR NOTES

THE BIBLE

The Bible is how God speaks to us today[33]

- It is God's own words written down by holy men who were chosen by God and taught by the Holy Spirit.[34]

The Bible tells how man rebelled against God[35] and how He sent His Son to save lost sinners[36]

- To save us from the terrible consequences of that rebellion, the day of God's wrath and judgment.[37]

The Bible is a true guide to heaven[38]

- It is truth and wisdom.[39]
- It never contradicts itself.[40]
- It contains everything we need for life and godliness.[41]

The Bible teaches us how to live to please God[42]

- It teaches us what sin is, as well as the behavior and attitudes which honor God.[43]
- To know how to live for God and resist the devil, we should read and meditate daily on what the Bible teaches.[44]

BIBLE REFERENCES

33   2 Tim 3:16-17   "All Scripture is God-breathed and is useful for teaching, rebuking, correcting and training in righteousness, so that the man of God may be thoroughly equipped for every good work." Also 2 Peter 1:19-21.

34   2 Peter 1:20-21   "Above all, you must understand that no prophecy of Scripture came about by the prophet's own interpretation. For prophecy never had its origin in the will of man, but men spoke from God as they were carried along by the Holy Spirit." Also I Cor 2:13

35   Gen 6:5-6   "The Lord saw how great man's wickedness on the earth had become, and that every inclination of the thoughts of his heart was only evil all the time. The Lord was grieved that he had made man on the earth, and his heart was filled with pain." Also I Cor 10:1-10

36   John 3:16   "For God so loved the world that he gave his one and only Son, that whoever believes in him shall not perish but have eternal life." Also I Tim 1:15; Luke 19:10; Rom 5:8

37   Rom 5:9-10   "Since we have now been justified by his blood, how much more shall we be saved from God's wrath through him! For if, when we were God's enemies, we were reconciled to him through the death of his Son, how much more, having been reconciled, shall we be saved through his life!" Also Matt 25:31-46

38   John 5:24   "I tell you the truth, whoever hears my word and believes him who sent me has eternal life and will not be condemned; he has crossed over from death to life."

      2 Tim 3:15   "And how from infancy you have known the holy Scriptures, which are able to make you wise for salvation through faith in Christ Jesus." Also Eph 1:13

39   John 17:17   "Sanctify them by the truth; your word is truth." Also Col 2:2-3; Eph 1:13

40   2 Sam 22:31   "As for God, his way is perfect; the word of the Lord is flawless. He is a shield for all who take refuge in him." Also James 1:25

41   2 Peter 1:3   "His divine power has given us everything we need for life and godliness through our knowledge of him who called us by his own glory and goodness."

      2 Tim 3:16-17   "All Scripture is God-breathed and is useful for teaching, rebuking, correcting and training in righteousness, so that the man of God may be thoroughly equipped for every good work."

42   2 Tim 3:16-17   "All Scripture is God-breathed and is useful for teaching, rebuking, correcting and training in righteousness, so that the man of God may be thoroughly equipped for every good work." Also Eph 1:13-14

43   Gal 5:19-21   "The acts of the sinful nature are obvious: sexual immorality, impurity and debauchery; idolatry and witchcraft; hatred, discord, jealously, fits of rage, selfish ambition, dissensions, factions and envy; drunkenness, orgies, and the like. I warn you, as I did before, that those who live like this will not inherit the kingdom of God." Also Eph 4:17-5:21

44   Deut. 6:6-7 "These commandments that I give you today are to be upon your hearts. Impress them on your children. Talk about them when you sit at home and when you walk along the road, when you lie down and when you get up."

      James 1:21   "Therefore, get rid of all moral filth and the evil that is so prevalent and humbly accept the word planted in you, which can save you." Also Col 3:16; Eph 6:10-18; Psalm 1

WRITE DOWN YOUR THOUGHTS

SIN

Sin is living to please self[45] instead of living to please God[46]

- We sin when we don't live according to God's moral will for our lives.[47]
- Sin includes things we think, say and do as well as things we should do, but don't.[48]

God is greatly displeased when we are not careful to obey everything He commands us to do[49]

- Since Adam and Eve sinned, all of us are born with a sinful nature. That means we want to seek after our own pleasure instead of serving God.[50]
- God hates pride, selfishness and unthankfulness.[51]
- Sin brings on God's just wrath and punishment.[52]

All people have sinned and fall short of God's requirements to enter heaven[53]

- Sin separates us from God and makes us His enemies.[54]

God is a fair, but strict, judge[55]

- He knows our thoughts and secrets, and nothing we do can be hidden from Him.[56]
- God never forgets.[57]
- He will judge each person according to his sin.[58]

God's punishment for our sin is death[59]...

- All people die.[60]

and never ending suffering in the fire of hell[61]

- Hell is God's garbage dump for ruined people.[62]
- In hell people will experience terrible pain, darkness, hopelessness and loneliness forever and ever.[63]
- Hell separates us from everything that is good and enjoyable.[64]

We are unable to repay God for our sins[65]

- We cannot save ourselves no matter what we do.[66]
- There is nothing we have that God doesn't already own.[67]

The *good news* is that God offers us a way to be saved[68]

- Gospel means "good news".[69]
- In His mercy God has provided a way for those who trust in Him to be perfectly righteous in His sight, completely forgiven, and saved from hell.[70]

If we accept His offer, we will one day go to heaven[71]

- God offers to rescue us.[72]
- Heaven is filled with joy, beauty, comfort, peace and love. There is no sin, loneliness or sorrow there.[73]
- Even the most wonderful things on earth cannot compare to the beauty and awesomeness of heaven.[74]
- We will be with our loving God in new, perfect bodies without sickness, hunger or pain.[75]

BIBLE REFERENCES

45   Rom 2:8 "But for those who are self-seeking and who reject the truth and follow evil, there will be wrath and anger." Also 1 John 2:15-16; 2 Tim 3:1-5

46   Eph 2:3 "All of us also lived among them at one time, gratifying the cravings of our sinful nature and following its desires and thoughts. Like the rest, we were by nature objects of wrath."

47   Matt 7:21 "Not everyone who says to me, 'Lord, Lord,' will enter the kingdom of heaven, but only he who does the will of my Father who is in heaven."

48   Matt 5:21-22 "You have heard that it was said to the people long ago, 'Do not murder, and anyone who murders will be subject to judgment. But I tell you that anyone who is angry with his brother will be subject to judgment. Again, anyone who says to his brother, 'Raca,' is answerable to the Sanhedrin. But anyone who says, 'You fool!' will be in danger of the fire of hell." Also Luke 11:42; Rom 14:22-23; Prov 15:26

49   Rom 1:18 "The wrath of God is being revealed from heaven against all the godlessness and wickedness of men who suppress the truth by their wickedness." Also Psalm 5:4-6; James 2:10

50   Eph 2:3 "All of us also lived among them at one time, gratifying the cravings of our sinful nature and following its desires and thoughts. Like the rest, we were by nature objects of wrath." Also Rom 5:12

51   Prov 8:13 "To fear the Lord is to hate evil; I hate pride and arrogance, evil behavior and perverse speech." Prov 16:5 "The Lord detests all the proud of heart. Be sure of this: They will not go unpunished." Also Isa 13:9-13; Eph 2:3

52   Isa 13:9, 11 "See, the day of the Lord is coming – a cruel day, with wrath and fierce anger – to make the land desolate and destroy the sinners within it... I will punish the world for its evil, the wicked for their sins. I will put an end to the arrogance of the haughty and will humble the pride of the ruthless."

53   Rom 3:10-12 "There is no one righteous, not even one; there is no one who understands, no one who seeks God. All have turned away, they have together become worthless; there is no one who does good not even one." Also Gal 3:22; 1 John 1:8-10; Rom 5:12

54   Isa 59:2-3 "But your iniquities have separated you from your God; your sins have hidden his face from you, so that he will not hear. For your hands are stained with blood, your fingers with guilt. Your lips have spoken lies, and your tongue mutters wicked things."

55   Psalm 7:11"God is a righteous judge, a God who expresses his wrath every day." Also Psalm 96:10; Rom 2:5-6

56   Heb 4:13 "Nothing in all creation is hidden from God's sight. Everything is uncovered and laid bare before the eyes of him to whom we must give account."

57   Heb 6:10 "God is not unjust; he will not forget your work and the love you have shown him as you have helped his people and continue to help them."

58   Rom 2:6-8 "God will give to each person according to what he has done. To those who by persistence in doing good seek glory, honor and immortality, he will give eternal life. But for those who are self-seeking and who reject the truth and follow evil, there will be wrath and anger."

     Rom 2:11 "For God does not show favoritism." Also Acts 17:31; Deut 24:16

59   Rom 5:12 "Therefore, just as sin entered the world through one man, and death through sin, and in this way death came to all men, because all sinned." Also Eze 18:20; Gen 2:16-17

60   Psalm 89:48 "What man can live and not see death, or save himself from the power of the grave?" Also Rom 5:12

61   Mark 9:47-49 "And if your eye causes you to sin, pluck it out. It is better for you to enter the kingdom of God with one eye than to have two eyes and be thrown into hell, where 'their worm does not die, and the fire is not quenched.' Everyone will be salted with fire." Also 2 Thes 1:8-9

62   Isa 66:23-24 "'From one New Moon to another and from one Sabbath to another, all mankind will come and bow down before me,' says the Lord. 'And they will go out and look upon the dead bodies of those who rebelled against me; their worm will not die, nor will their fire be quenched, and they will be loathsome to all mankind." Matt 25:41 "Then he will say to those on his left, 'Depart from me, you who are cursed, into the eternal fire prepared for the devil and his angels.'"

63   Luke 16:24 "So he called to him, 'Father Abraham, have pity on me and send Lazarus to dip the tip of his finger in water and cool my tongue, because I am in agony in this fire.'"

Rev 20:10 "They will be tormented day and night for ever and ever." Also 2 Peter 2:17; Rev 21:8

64 Luke 16:26 "And besides all this, between us and you a great chasm has been fixed, so that those who want to go from here to you cannot, nor can anyone cross over from there to us."

2 Thes 1:8-9 "He will punish those who do not know God and do not obey the gospel of our Lord Jesus. They will be punished with everlasting destruction and shut out from the presence of the Lord and from the majesty of his power."

65 Titus 3:5 "He saved us, not because of righteous things we had done, but because of his mercy."

Rom 11:35 "Who has ever given to God, that God should repay him?"

66 Eph 2:1-3 "As for you, you were dead in your transgressions and sins, in which you used to live when you followed the ways of this world and of the ruler of the kingdom of the air, the spirit who is now at work in those who are disobedient." Also Luke 19:10

67 Neh 9:6 "You alone are the Lord. You made the heavens, even the highest heavens, and all their starry host, the earth and all that is on it, the seas and all that is in them. You give life to everything, and the multitudes of heaven worship you." Also Eze 18:4; 1 Cor. 4:7

68 John 6:40 "For my Father's will is that everyone who looks to the Son and believes in him shall have eternal life, and I will raise him up at the last day." Rom 1:16-17 "I am not ashamed of the gospel, because it is the power of God for the salvation of everyone who believes: first for the Jew, then for the Gentile. For in the gospel a righteousness from God is revealed, a righteousness that is by faith from first to last, just as it is written: 'The righteous will live by faith.'" Also Acts 4:12; Rom 5:8-10; Isa 55:6-7; Eze 18:30-32

69 Mark 1:14-15 "After John was put in prison, Jesus went into Galilee, proclaiming the good news of God. 'The time has come,' he said. 'The kingdom of God is near. Repent and believe the good news!'" Also Eph 1:13

70 Rom 1:16-17 "I am not ashamed of the gospel, because it is the power of God for the salvation of everyone who believes: first for the Jew, then for the Gentile. For in the gospel a righteousness from God is revealed, a righteousness that is by faith from first to last, just as it is written: 'The righteous will live by faith.'"

71 John 3:16 "For God so loved the world that he gave his one and only Son, that whoever believes in him shall not perish but have eternal live."

1 Thes 4:16-17 "For the Lord himself will come down from heaven, with a loud command, with the voice of the archangel and with the trumpet call of God, and the dead in Christ will rise first. After that, we who are still alive and are left will be caught up together with them in the clouds to meet the Lord in the air. And so we will be with the Lord forever."

72 Gal 1:3-4 "Grace and peace to you from God our Father and the Lord Jesus Christ, who gave himself for our sins to rescue us from the present evil age, according to the will of our God and Father."

73 Rev 21:1 "Then I saw a new heaven and a new earth, for the first heaven and the first earth had passed away, and there was no longer any sea." Rev 21:4 "He will wipe every tear from their eyes. There will be no more death or mourning or crying or pain, for the old order of things has passed away." Also Rev 21:1-4; Rev 21:15-27; 1 Cor 2:9

74 Rev 21:18-21 "The wall was made of jasper, and the city of pure gold, as pure as glass. The foundations of the city walls were decorated with every kind of precious stone. The first foundation was jasper, the second sapphire, the third chalcedony, the fourth emerald, the fifth sardonyx, the sixth carnelian, the seventh chrysolite, the eighth beryl, the ninth topaz, the tenth chrysoprase, the eleventh jacinth, and the twelfth amethyst. The twelve gates were twelve pearls, each gate made of a single pearl. The great street of the city was of pure gold, like transparent glass."

75 Rev 21:3-4 "And I heard a loud voice from the throne saying, 'Now the dwelling of God is with men, and he will live with them. They will be his people, and God himself will be with them and be their God. He will wipe every tear from their eyes. There will be no more death or mourning or crying or pain, for the old order of things has passed away.'" Also Rev 21:22-23

WRITE DOWN YOUR THOUGHTS

JESUS

Jesus is God's own, dearly loved Son[76]

- By Him and for Him all things were created.[77]
- Jesus is fully God and fully man.[78]

Jesus came into the world to die for sinners and rescue them from hell[79]

- God requires sin to be paid for by the shedding of blood.[80]

Jesus was a man just like us[81]

- He had skin and bones like us.[82]
- He felt the good and bad things we feel.[83]
- He understands what hurts us and what makes us happy.[84]
- His mother was Mary; Joseph was His guardian; but His father was God.[85]

Although He was tempted like us, He <u>never</u> sinned[86]

- He perfectly kept God's whole law.[87]
- He spent His life loving God, honoring His parents, obeying the authorities, being kind, speaking truth, and humbly serving others.[88]
- He never sinned in thought, word, deed, or omission.[89]

Jesus willingly took on Himself the punishment we deserve for our sins[90]

- He did this out of love for those who would believe and trust in Him.[91]
- God laid the sins of those who would believe, on His innocent Son.[92]
- He suffered, bled and died in the place of all who would have faith in Him.[93]
- The punishment He received was horrible. He was insulted, shamed, beaten, spit upon, crowned with thorns, mocked, and died an agonizing death on the cross.[94]

All the wrath and punishment God had for believers' sins was used up on Jesus[95]

- Jesus' death completely satisfied God's justice.[96]
- God has no further complaint against anyone who believes in His Son. By trusting in Him our sins are fully paid for. We are completely forgiven.[97]
- God also took the record of Jesus' perfect life and credited it to our record in heaven.[98]
- Believers' past, present and future sins are forgiven, and we are adopted into the family of God as dearly loved children.[99]

Jesus rose from the dead[100]

- He died on the cross on Friday and was put in a tomb. On Sunday He came out of the grave **alive** in a new and perfect body.[101]
- He will never die again.[102]
- Over 500 people saw Jesus alive![103]
- His resurrection proved that God accepted His perfect sacrifice on the cross as payment for our sins.[104]

Jesus ascended into heaven[105]

- He went up to be with God His Father.[106]
- He is now seated on the throne as King of kings.[107]
- He is alive today, working so that those who love Him can come to heaven to be with Him forever.[108]
- Satan has been defeated and will soon be destroyed forever.[109]

Jesus is coming back again[110]

- Some day, perhaps in the near future, those who love Jesus will, in a flash, receive new bodies and ascend to meet Him when He returns.[111]
- He will take those who love Him to heaven and bring terrible punishment on those who reject Him as Lord and King.[112]
- This world will be consumed in fire and a new heaven and a new earth will be created where there is no sin or sorrow at all.[113]

BIBLE REFERENCES

76 Matt 3:16-17 "As soon as Jesus was baptized, he went up out of the water. At that moment heaven was opened, and he saw the Spirit of God descending like a dove and lighting on him. And a voice from heaven said, 'This is my Son, whom I love; with him I am well pleased.'" Also Col 2:9-10; Gal 4:4

77 Col 1:16 "For by him all things were created: things in heaven and on earth, visible and invisible, whether thrones or powers or rulers or authorities; all things were created by him and for him."

78 Col 1:19 "For God was pleased to have all his fullness dwell in him."

Heb 2:14-15 "Since the children have flesh and blood, he too shared in their humanity so that by his death he might destroy him who holds the power of death – that is, the devil – and free those who all their lives were held in slavery by their fear of death." Also Gal 4:4

79 Rom 5:8 "But God demonstrates his own love for us in this: While we were still sinners, Christ died for us." Gal 1:3-4 "... and Jesus Christ, who gave himself for our sins to rescue us from the present evil age ..." Also I Tim 1:15; John 6:38-40

80 Heb 9:22 "...and without the shedding of blood there is no forgiveness."

81 Heb 2:14 "Since the children have flesh and blood, he too shared in their humanity so that by his death he might destroy him who holds the power of death – that is, the devil." Also Luke 24:39

82 Luke 24:39 "Look at my hands and my feet. It is I myself! Touch me and see; a ghost does not have flesh and bones, as you see I have."

83 Heb 4:15 "For we do not have a high priest who is unable to sympathize with our weaknesses, but we have one who has been tempted in every way, just as we are – yet was without sin."

Heb 5:2 "He is able to deal gently with those who are ignorant and are going astray, since he himself is subject to weakness."

84 Please read Isaiah 53:1-12

85 Matt 1:18 "This is how the birth of Jesus Christ came about: His mother Mary was pledged to be married to Joseph, but before they came together, she was found to be with child through the Holy Spirit."

86 Heb 4:15 "For we do not have a high priest who is unable to sympathize with our weaknesses, but we have one who has been tempted in every way, just as we are – yet was without sin." Also Heb 2:18; 1 Peter 2:22; 2 Cor 5:21

87 Matt. 5:17 "Do not think that I have come to abolish the Law or the Prophets; I have not come to abolish them but to fulfill them." 2 Cor 5:21 "God made him who had no sin to be sin for us, so that in him we might become the righteousness of God." Also Rom 5:19; Heb 7:26; 1 Peter 2:22

88 Heb 7:26 "Such a high priest meets our need – one who is holy, blameless, pure, set apart from sinners, exalted above the heavens."

89 I Peter 2:22-23 "He committed no sin, and no deceit was found in his mouth. When they hurled their insults at him, he did not retaliate; when he suffered, he made no threats. Instead, he entrusted himself to him who judges justly."

90 John 10:17-18 "The reason my Father loves me is that I lay down my life – only to take it up again. No one takes it from me, but I lay it down of my own accord. I have authority to lay it down and authority to take it up again."

I Peter 2:24 "He himself bore our sins in his body on the tree, so that we might die to sins and live for righteousness; by his wounds you have been healed." Also Isa 53:5-6

91 John 3:16 "For God so loved the world that he gave his one and only Son, that whoever believes in him shall not perish but have eternal life." Also I John 3:16; I John 4:10

92 Isa 53:6 "We all, like sheep, have gone astray, each of us has turned to his own way; and the Lord has laid on him the iniquity of us all."

Rom 3:22 "This righteousness from God comes through faith in Jesus Christ to all who believe." Also Rom 3:21-26; 1 John 4:10; Isa 53:10-11

93 1 Peter 2:24 "He himself bore our sins in his body on the tree, so that we might die to sins and live for righteousness; by his wounds you have been healed." Also Heb 2:10

94 Isa 52:14 "Just as there were many who were appalled at him – his appearance was so disfigured beyond that of any man and his form marred beyond human likeness."

Isa 53:5 "But he was pierced for our transgressions, he was crushed for our iniquities; the punishment that brought us peace was upon him, and by his wounds we are healed." Also Matt 26:57-27:56; Mark 14:65; Mark 15:1-41

95 Isa 53:5-6 "But he was pierced for our transgressions, he was crushed for our iniquities; the punishment that brought us peace was upon him, and by his wounds we are healed. We all, like sheep, have gone astray, each of us has turned to his own way; and the Lord has laid on him the iniquity of us all." Also Isa 53:10-11; Rom 8:3

96 Rom 3:25-26 "God presented him as a sacrifice of atonement, through faith in his blood. He did this to demonstrate his justice, because in his forbearance he had left the sins committed beforehand unpunished – he did it to demonstrate his justice at the present time, so as to be just and the one who justifies those who have faith in Jesus." Also Heb 10:14-18

97 Rom 5:8-10 "But God demonstrates his own love for us in this: While we were still sinners, Christ died for us. Since we have now been justified by his blood, how much more shall we be saved from God's wrath through him! For if, when we were God's enemies, we were reconciled to him through the death of his Son, how much more, having been reconciled, shall we be saved through his life."   Also Heb 10:17-18

98 Rom 5:18-19 "Consequently, just as the result of one trespass was condemnation for all men, so also the result of one act of righteousness was justification that brings life for all men. For just as through the disobedi-ence of the one man the many were made sinners, so also through the obedience of the one man the many will be made righteous." Also Rom 3:21-24

99 I John 3:1 "How great is the love the Father has lavished on us, that we should be called children of God! And that is what we are!" Also Eph 1:3-8; Eph 5:1-2

100 Luke 24:46-47 "He told them, 'This is what is written: The Christ will suffer and rise from the dead on the third day, and repentance and forgiveness of sins will be preached in his name to all nations, begin-ning at Jerusalem." Also Luke 24:7; 1 Cor 15:3-4

101 Luke 24:1 "On the first day of the week, very early in the morning, the women took the spices they had prepared and went to the tomb."

Luke 24:5-6 "Why do you look for the living among the dead? He is not here; he has risen!"

102 Rom 6:9 "For we know that since Christ was raised from the dead, he cannot die again; death no longer has mastery over him."

103 I Cor 15:5-6 "He appeared to Peter, and then to the twelve. After that, he appeared to more than five hun-dred of the brothers at the same time."

104 Rom 4:25 "He was delivered over to death for our sins and was raised to life for our justification."

Acts 13:37-39 "But the one whom God raised from the dead did not see decay. Therefore, my brothers, I want you to know that through Jesus the forgiveness of sins is proclaimed to you. Through him everyone who believes is justified from everything you could not be justified from by the law of Moses." Also Eph 1:19-23

105 Luke 24:50-51 "When he had led them out to the vicinity of Bethany, he lifted up his hands and blessed them. While he was blessing them, he left them and was taken up into heaven." Also Acts 1:9

106 Eph 1:20 "He raised him from the dead and seated him at his right hand in the heavenly realms." Also Heb 1:3

107 Rev 17:14 "They will make war against the Lamb, but the Lamb will overcome them because he is Lord of lords and King of kings – and with him will be his called, chosen and faithful followers." Also Eph 1:21-22; Phil 2:9-11

108 John 14:2-3 "In my Father's house are many rooms; if it were not so, I would have told you. I am going there to prepare a place for you. And if I go and prepare a place for you, I will come back and take you to be with me that you also may be where I am." Also Heb 7:24-25

109 I John 3:8 "The reason the Son of God appeared was to destroy the devil's work."

Rev 20:10 "And the devil, who deceived them, was thrown into the lake of burning sulfur, where the beast and the false prophet had been thrown. They will be tormented day and night for ever and ever." Also Rom 16:20

110 Rev 22:12 "Behold, I am coming soon! My reward is with me, and I will give to everyone according to what he has done." Also Acts 1:11

111 I Thes 4:16-17 "For the Lord himself will come down from heaven, with a loud command, with the voice of the archangel and with the trumpet call of God, and the dead in Christ will rise first. After that, we who are still alive and are left will be caught up together with them in the clouds to meet the Lord in the air. And so we will be with the Lord forever." Also I Cor 15:51-52

112 Matt 25:34 "Then the King will say to those on his right, 'Come, you who are blessed by my Father; take your inheritance, the kingdom prepared for you since the creation of the world."

Matt 25:41 "Then he will say to those on his left, 'Depart from me, you who are cursed, into the eternal fire prepared for the devil and his angels.'"

113 2 Peter 3:10, 12-13 "But the day of the Lord will come like a thief. The heavens will disappear with a roar; the elements will be destroyed by fire, and the earth and everything in it will be laid bare. . . That day will bring about the destruction of the heavens by fire, and the elements will melt in the heat. But in keeping with his promise we are looking forward to a new heaven and a new earth, the home of righteousness."

WRITE DOWN YOUR THOUGHTS

REPENTANCE & FAITH

God's offer of forgiveness comes through repentance[114] and faith[115]

- This offer of forgiveness is known as salvation[116] or redemption.[117]

Repentance means turning away from our selfish, sinful lives[118]

- Repentance means being deeply sorry for offending our holy, good and loving God.[119]
- We must confess our sins to God in prayer as we come to know them, and resolve by the grace of God not to commit them again.[120]
- God will enable us, in time, to escape from the control that sin has had over our lives.[121]
- He is very patient, faithful and gentle.[122]

Faith means believing and relying upon the Lord Jesus Christ alone[123]

- We must believe He is who the Bible says He is.[124]
- We must trust that He will do what the Bible says He will do.[125]

We must learn to place <u>all</u> our trust in Jesus to make us right with God[126]

- God's forgiveness is not deserved and cannot be earned or bought.[127]
- We must not trust in ourselves or what we do to gain God's acceptance.[128]
- By trusting in Jesus alone, we are adopted as dearly loved children,[129] and God the Holy Spirit will guide us on the narrow path that leads to heaven.[130]

BIBLE REFERENCES

114 Acts 17:30 "In the past God overlooked such ignorance, but now he commands all people everywhere to repent." Also Matt 4:17

115 Rom 3:21-22 "But now a righteousness from God, apart from law, has been made known, to which the Law and the Prophets testify. This righteousness from God comes through faith in Jesus Christ to all who believe." Also Rom 1:17

116 Rom 1:16 "I am not ashamed of the gospel, because it is the power of God for the salvation of everyone who believes."

117 Eph 1:7 "In him we have redemption through his blood, the forgiveness of sins, in accordance with the riches of God's grace."

118 Eze 18:21-22 "But if a wicked man turns away from all the sins he has committed and keeps all my decrees and does what is just and right, he will surely live; he will not die. None of the offenses he has committed will be remembered against him."

Acts 3:19 "Repent, then, and turn to God, so that your sins may be wiped out, that times of refreshing may come from the Lord." Also Isa 55:6-7

119 2 Cor 7:10 "Godly sorrow brings repentance that leads to salvation and leaves no regret."

120 I John 1:9 "If we confess our sins, he is faithful and just and will forgive us our sins and purify us from all unrighteousness." Also Acts 3:19

121 2 Peter 1:3-4 "His divine power has given us everything we need for life and godliness through our knowledge of him who called us by his own glory and goodness."

122 Matt 11:28-30 "Come to me, all you who are weary and burdened, and I will give you rest. Take my yoke upon you and learn from me, for I am gentle and humble in heart, and you will find rest for your souls. For my yoke is easy and my burden is light." Also Matt 12:20

123 John 3:36 "Whoever believes in the Son has eternal life, but whoever rejects the Son will not see life, for God's wrath remains on him."

Acts 4:12 "Salvation is found in no one else, for there is no other name under heaven given to men by which we must be saved." Also Heb 11:6

124 John 5:24 ""I tell you the truth, whoever hears my word and believes him who sent me has eternal life and will not be condemned; he has crossed over from death to life."

Gal 4:4-5 "But when the time had fully come, God sent his Son, born of a woman, born under law, to redeem those under law, that we might receive the full rights of sons." Also Col 1:15-20; John 20:31

125 John 6:38-40 "For I have come down from heaven not to do my will but to do the will of him who sent me. And this is the will of him who sent me, that I shall lose none of all that he has given me, but raise them up at the last day. For my Father's will is that everyone who looks to the Son and believes in him shall have eternal life, and I will raise him up at the last day." Also John 14:1-3; John 20:31

126 John 14:1-3 "Do not let your hearts be troubled. Trust in God; trust also in me. In my Father's house are many rooms; if it were not so, I would have told you. I am going there to prepare a place for you. And if I go and prepare a place for you, I will come back and take you to be with me that you also may be where I am." Also Jude 1:24-25; Rom 8:1-2

127 Eph 2:8-9 "For it is by grace you have been saved, through faith – and this not from yourselves, it is the gift of God – not by works, so that no one can boast." Also Isa 55:1-3; Rom 9:16

128 Eph 2:1-3 "As for you, you were dead in your transgressions and sins, in which you used to live when you followed the ways of this world and of the ruler of the kingdom of the air, the spirit who is now at work in those who are disobedient. All of us also lived among them at one time, gratifying the cravings of our sinful nature and following its desires and thoughts. Like the rest, we were by nature objects of wrath." Also 2 Tim 1:9; Isa 64:6

129 I John 3:1 "How great is the love the Father has lavished on us, that we should be called children of God! And that is what we are! The reason the world does not know us is that it did not know him." Also Rom 8:16-17

130 Rom 8:13-14 "For if you live according to the sinful nature, you will die; but if by the Spirit you put to death the misdeeds of the body, you will live, because those who are led by the Spirit of God are sons of God."

John 16:13 "But when he, the Spirit of truth, comes, he will guide you into all truth. He will not speak on his own; he will speak only what he hears, and he will tell you what is yet to come." Also Matt 7:13-14; Gal 5:16

WRITE DOWN YOUR THOUGHTS

COUNTING THE COSTS

Before we begin to follow Jesus we must consider the cost[131]

- Jesus does not want disciples who are not willing to follow Him with all their heart.[132]
- We must give rightful control of our lives back to God and live according to His revealed moral will.[133]
- We should be baptized in the name of Jesus Christ.[134]
- We must not imitate ungodly behavior to gain acceptance from others.[135]
- Jesus must be the number **one** priority in our lives above absolutely everything else. He must be the center of our affections.[136]
- We must be willing to follow Him till the end of our life.[137]

We will be persecuted[138]

- Believers will be persecuted in this world for their faith. But God promises never to leave us and never to give us more than we can handle.[139]
- Many people will think you are strange for not going along with their sinful ways. You must be prepared to turn the other cheek when people insult you.[140]

Those who choose to follow Jesus will have an abundant, joyful life in this world and the indescribable wonders of heaven in the next[141]

- The Christian's hope is in heaven, not in this world, but Jesus also says that our life here will be abundant and full of joy.[142]
- The inner peace and joy in this life,[143] as well as the rewards of heaven, will far outweigh all the difficulties Christians face.[144]
- As God's adopted children we are heirs with Christ to the glories of heaven.[145]

BIBLE REFERENCES

131   I Peter 4:18 "If it is hard for the righteous to be saved, what will become of the ungodly and the sinner?" Also Luke 14:26-33; Matt. 5:3-12

132   Mark 12:30 "Love the Lord your God with all your heart and with all your soul and with all your mind and with all your strength."

Matt 10:37-39 "Anyone who loves his father or mother more than me is not worthy of me; anyone who loves his son or daughter more than me is not worthy of me; and anyone who does not take his cross and follow me is not worthy of me. Whoever finds his life will lose it, and whoever loses his life for my sake will find it." Also Luke 9:62

133   Matt 7:21 "Not everyone who says to me, 'Lord, Lord,' will enter the kingdom of heaven, but only he who does the will of my Father who is in heaven." Also I Cor 6:19-20; Rom 12:1-2

134   Acts 2:38 "Repent and be baptized, every one of you, in the name of Jesus Christ for the forgiveness of your sins. And you will receive the gift of the Holy Spirit."

135   James 4:4 ". . . don't you know that friendship with the world is hatred toward God? Anyone who chooses to be a friend of the world becomes an enemy of God." Also Prov 1:8-19; Eph 5:1-7; I John 2:15-17

136   Matt 10:37-39 "Anyone who loves his father or mother more than me is not worthy of me; anyone who loves his son or daughter more than me is not worthy of me; and anyone who does not take his cross and follow me is not worthy of me. Whoever finds his life will lose it, and whoever loses his life for my sake will find it." Also John 14:23; Matt 22:37-38

137   Col 1:22-23 "But now he has reconciled you by Christ's physical body through death to present you holy in his sight, without blemish and free from accusation – if you continue in your faith, established and firm, not moved from the hope held out in the gospel."

Matt 10:22 "All men will hate you because of me, but he who stands firm to the end will be saved." Also Heb 10:35-36

138   Rom 8:17 "Now if we are children, then we are heirs – heirs of God and co-heirs with Christ, if indeed we share in his sufferings in order that we may also share in his glory." Also Matt 5:10-12; I Peter 4:12-16

139   Heb 13:5-6 ". . . God has said, 'Never will I leave you; never will I forsake you.' So we say with confidence, 'The Lord is my helper; I will not be afraid. What can man do to me?'"

I Cor 10:13 "No temptation has seized you except what is common to man. And God is faithful; he will not let you be tempted beyond what you can bear. But when you are tempted, he will also provide a way out so that you can stand up under it."

140   Luke 6:29 "If someone strikes you on one cheek, turn to him the other also. If someone takes your cloak, do not stop him from taking your tunic."

Luke 6:22-23 "Blessed are you when men hate you, when they exclude you and insult you and reject your name as evil, because of the Son of Man. Rejoice in that day and leap for joy, because great is your reward in heaven."

141   John 10:10 ". . . I have come that they may have life, and have it to the full."

I Cor 2:9 "No eye has seen, no ear has heard, no mind has conceived what God has prepared for those who love him."

142   Matt 19:29 "And everyone who has left houses or brothers or sisters or father or mother or children or fields for my sake will receive a hundred times as much and will inherit eternal life." Also Rom 14:17; I Peter 1:3-9; Jude 1:24

143   I Peter 1:8-9 "Though you have not seen him, you love him; and even though you do not see him now, you believe in him and are filled with an inexpressible and glorious joy, for you are receiving the goal of your faith, the salvation of your souls." Also Gal 5:22-23

144   John 14:1-3 "Do not let your hearts be troubled. Trust in God; trust also in me. In my Father's house are many rooms; if it were not so, I would have told you. And if I go and prepare a place for you, I will come back and take you to be with me that you also may be where I am." Also I Peter 1:3-9; Jude 1:24-25

145   Rom 8:16-17 "The Spirit himself testifies with our spirit that we are God's children. Now if we are children, then we are heirs – heirs of God and co-heirs with Christ, if indeed we share in his sufferings in order that we may also share in his glory." Also Gal 4:6-7

WRITE DOWN YOUR THOUGHTS

ABBREVIATION KEY

OLD TESTAMENT

2 Sam = Second Samuel
Dan = Daniel
Deut = Deuteronomy
Eccl = Ecclesiastes
Eze = Ezekiel
Gen = Genesis
Isa = Isaiah
Jer = Jeremiah
Job = Job
Lev = Leviticus
Neh = Nehemiah
Prov = Proverbs
Psalm = Psalms

NEW TESTAMENT

Acts = Acts
Col = Colossians
I Cor = First Corinthians
2 Cor = Second Corinthians
Eph = Ephesians
Gal = Galatians
Heb = Hebrews
James = James
John = John
I John = First John
Jude = Jude
Luke = Luke
Mark = Mark
Matt = Matthew
I Peter = First Peter
2 Peter = Second Peter
Phil = Philippians
Rev = Revelation
Rom = Romans
I Thes = First Thessalonians
2 Thes = Second Thessalonians
I Tim = First Timothy
2 Tim = Second Timothy
Titus = Titus

THE GOSPEL SUMMARIZED

God the Father, Son and Holy Spirit is one God, self existent, eternal, all powerful and perfect, the creator of all things. God is fair and just and works out everything, even to the smallest detail, in conformity with the purpose of His will.

God created the first man and woman, Adam and Eve, in His own likeness. He created them to glorify Himself through a wonderful intimate relationship, lived out in perfect obedience, contentment, joy and mutual love.

But Adam and Eve sinned against their loving Father and creator and, in so doing, completely destroyed their ability, and the ability of all their children (us), to have a right relationship with God.

The Bible, along with our own experience, illustrates the terrible consequences of that first sin of disobedience. Men do terrible acts against their God and each other. The Bible teaches that *all* men are born with a corrupt, selfish nature and, in relation to God, are *dead* because of their sins.

The consequence of this is that upon death men are separated from God and all that is good forever. The place of separation, called *hell*, is filled with darkness, pain and eternal torment. But because of His mercy, love and compassion, our God, who is perfectly just, has also provided a *way* for lost sinners to be right with Him that does not depend on the gross inadequacy of our own works.

The way of salvation that God provided is through the work of *Jesus Christ*, His beloved son. Jesus became man and lived a life of perfect obedience. He willingly took upon Himself our sin and received the full measure of punishment that that sin required, thereby satisfying God's holy justice.

God has promised that whoever believes in His son, turns in repentance away from his sin and places all his trust in Jesus' perfect life and substitutionary sacrifice on his behalf, *will be <u>saved</u>!* Jesus took the punishment we deserve and freely credits the righteousness He merited to our account in heaven.

All who accept God's free offer of salvation by faith in Christ are *adopted* into His royal family, live under the benefits of His kingdom on earth, and are *heirs* together with Christ to the indescribable glories of heaven in the next.

We implore you on Christ's behalf: Be reconciled to God! God made Him who had no sin to be sin for us, so that in Him we might become the righteousness of God (2 Cor. 5:20-21).

WHAT NEXT?

Having our children embrace Jesus Christ as Lord and Savior based on a clear knowledge of the Gospel is the most important concern of a Christian parent. Jesus said, "Let the little children come to me and do not hinder them, for the kingdom of heaven belongs to such as these" (Matt. 19:14). But, we must at the same time recognize that in our zealousness to see our children saved we can subtly pressure them into making a decision to follow Christ in order to please us, rather than God who knows the heart. The consequences of a profession of faith made under pressure, and not from a sincere heart can be serious, and in time can bring confusion and sorrow to everyone involved. For this reason it is suggested that once a child learns the Gospel, parents should on occasion let the child know that if he desires to talk about the things of salvation, they would always be happy to do so.

Our responsibility is to encourage our children to come to Christ while they are still young. However, salvation is of the Lord, and we must be willing to patiently wait on God.

Should your child come to show a real interest in the things of God, giving evidence of God's transforming grace in his life, demonstrated by conviction of and repentance for sin, an affectionate desire to live to please Jesus and a willingness to obediently follow Christ despite the cost, then rejoice! Your child has likely been saved.

If so, as a new creation, he or she will be enabled by the Holy Spirit to live a life more and more pleasing to God. We ought to encourage and pray with our children that God will cause them to grow in the Christian graces and obedience to His Will as found in the Bible.

For more extensive information about this subject, I suggest you acquire the helpful little booklet, *Your Child's Profession of Faith*, by Dennis Gundersen (available through *GRACE & TRUTH BOOKS www.graceandtruthbooks.com*) as well as *Shepherding A Child's Heart* by Dr. Tedd Tripp.

MEMORY HELPS

MEMORY HELPS

Genesis · ISBN 978-0-9723046-0-3 · $16
Exodus · ISBN 978-0-9723046-1-0 · $14
Leviticus · ISBN 978-0-9723046-2-7 · $11
Numbers · ISBN 978-0-9767582-2-8 · $13

Numbers
Now
Available

Herein is Love

DEVOTIONAL SERIES FOR CHILDREN

- WRITTEN IN STORY FORM
- A RICH RESOURCE FOR TEACHING
- GREAT FOR FAMILY DEVOTIONS OR SUNDAY SCHOOL
- EACH VOLUME PROVIDES A COMPLETE TEACHER'S GUIDE

Bring God's redemptive story to life for your kids with the story of the Old Testament. Your own faith will be strengthened while reading to your children, and your children will be encouraged to believe in the Lord Jesus.

 SHEPHERD PRESS

40